FEEDING THE MASSES

Part 1 of a 3 part series

BY

DAVID T. MACFARLANE

This book is dedicated to:

The Scientist

Without You, There Would Be No

R&D

"Feed the Kings,

Eat with the masses.

Feed the masses,

Eat with the Kings."

Foodservice Proverb

I have written this series in an effort to help chefs who are or who are thinking of becoming product developers.

This book is part 1 of a 3 part series that personally, I think fills a need for information in order to help draw more talent and interest into this fantastic work.

Whenever I am asked why I decided to become a corporate chef, the answer is always an easy one. I chose this path in my culinary career so that the food that I help develop reaches as many people as possible.

One of the greatest rewards of developing food is the mere fact that the finished product doesn't discriminate. It's neither pretentious nor exclusive to catering only to the 1%. It mostly is attainable to anybody, regardless of social economic class, who enjoys good food.

I take what I do very seriously and I do admit that I am a bit of a perfectionist. I prefer the product to be developed properly. To go through a systematic check list of sorts ensuring the end product looks, tastes, functions and performs the way it is intended.

Regardless of your culinary training, product development will expose your strengths and weaknesses beyond imagination but like any aspect of cooking, preparation is paramount to success.

Everything a chef does starts with a prep list. That prep list not only has to be written properly but also has to be followed without equivocation. The prep list is by far essential to not only your success but also the success of the operation you are a part of. Although looked at by some as a time consuming menial task, it is just as important as the cooking, expediting and serving of any dish.

The same is true for prepared foods. They all start with what is known as the 'Gold Standard'. This gold standard is then meant to be the model of which you replicate as a manufactured finished good. The goal is to develop the finished good as close to the gold standard as possible.

As a chef, this is where the preparation comes in. Using all of your training whether from school or real life experience and understanding how to prepare the gold standard, could hinge on not only the success of the product but most importantly the success of the company.

It is imperative that the corporate chef not only executes the gold standard perfectly but is also highly capable of following direction to the letter. The corporate chef is an important part of the whole development process working in tandem with the marketing, food science and operational teams.

The intentions of this book are to give the reader an inside look at the work of a corporate chef. How the discipline has developed into helping prepared foods be better today than they have ever been in previous years.

The chef's role in the process has also expanded from just making the gold standard to working within the whole process till the end. The chef gives credibility to the project as well as prepares and presents the companies capabilities to broad audiences at trade shows, sales calls and industry meetings.

If you look at the options you have in the grocery store or your favorite chain restaurant there is a drawing awareness to chef inspired meals. Most companies capitalize on having these chefs develop their brands and reach the culinary astute public of today. These are the chefs I work with each day and they all demonstrate the importance of why they do it. It is to feed the masses.

Many corporations take pride in having a full time culinary staff on board and exploit it, as they should, to its maximum reach in a best effort to demonstrate their commitment to culinary excellence, expertise and innovation.

As a corporate chef, you have to be proficient to meet these deliverables. Excellence, expertise and innovation are non-negotiable when the lively hoods of hundreds or even thousands of people are depending on these to maximize sales.

As a corporate chef, you must be marketable. You will never see an advertisement saying, "Here's Chef So and So and he knows a little of what we do and tried his best through a limited education to create this!"

Instead, you will be touted as 'best in class' and put out there to not only bring credibility to the brand but be a resource to the customer. You need to be comfortable in this role. If you're not, it is doom and gloom ahead!

You will also have to get familiar with using lab equipment and terminology. Just as the classical French terminology was drilled into your eager little head back in culinary school, you will need to learn the many different terms associated with product development.

If you think back to middle school science class, you will begin to understand what I am talking about. With terms like specific gravity, water migration and viscosity it is really quite simple to understand and work through. Don't be intimidated by it all, especially if it is new to you. I would suggest taking an inventory of your lab equipment and tools then write down what they do and how best to use it. A PH meter will take more time to learn about than a bostwick so take your time and ask for help if needed.

The same goes for the plant equipment. Study it and get familiar with being comfortably proficient operating the machines and dialing in the settings. You will need to know this especially when leading plant trials and giving the line operators direction on the process and procedure. They are not going to listen to you if you don't know what you're talking about.

CHAPTER 1

OVERCOMING STEREOTYPES

Whenever I talk with culinary students today almost none of them know anything about the world of the corporate chef. Most are focused on graduating, interning at a high end restaurant that they will never afford to eat at then move on to a hotel corporate job or open their own 45 cover joint in hopes of getting a mention in a food column or magazine. They typically never consider going into a food manufacturing facility and develop a meal that will be fully prepared, frozen and produced at a rate of 80 per minute.

That's a good thing in my opinion, since the experience you attain from the fore mentioned gives you the ability to execute the later mentioned more perfectly. I say go, get it out of your system while your young and gain the experience necessary to develop those frozen prepared meals with the very best ideas and ingredients only after you discover that mass production is right for you.

If you think being a corporate chef is a 9 – 5 job to stay in the food business then nothing could be further from the truth. Sure it beats getting your rear end kicked during a Saturday night dinner rush where stress, heat and noise have laid victor over many an inspiring chef; it is never just a job.

It requires discipline beyond imagination as well as an innovative thought and an impeccable ability to be process driven all while recording and analyzing data to enhance the diners experience becomes the order of the day. It is a relentless schedule of flights, marathon test runs, product specification deadlines that becomes your dinner rush. Unfortunately this rush doesn't last only 2 ½ hours. It is indefinite.

If you think running an independent single unit restaurant is difficult as a chef then you would definitely have difficulty running 600 units as the chef. The stress is 600 times greater but so also are the rewards.

The first time I walked into a full scale production facility, I was overwhelmed. I could not believe the size of the equipment or the size of each batch being prepared. I was intimidated by what I didn't know as I watched the orchestration of mix, deposit and package being pulled off flawlessly.

It had been a long time since I ever felt so utterly useless to an operation. Having come from an executive chef role in a large hotel, it took me some time to get my bearings.

The one thing I had working in my favor was the fact that I ran bakery operations twice in my career, which I loved doing, but felt an obligation to fulfill my dream as a culinary student to be the chef of a hotel.

As a teenager, I was fortunate enough to learn the baking trade as an apprentice through vocational training. This training has paid dividends throughout my R&D career especially since baking is precise and so is R&D.

I overcame that feeling of intimidation the same way I did as a teenager, by learning the process. It is quite simply the process in which ingredients are measured and combined. The process of how the product is then shaped and carried through a system that enables consistency throughout the process to deliver a finished good that, after the quality check, is then packaged, cased and sent out for distribution.

The process I am talking about is one that helped me understand how the foods take shape. What the equipment was doing and most importantly why were the lines set up the way they were.

I wrote out on 2 sheets of paper the simultaneous efforts of 2 processes. 1, the paper on the left, described how I would make the product in my own kitchen. 2, the paper on the right, described how the production facility (plant) will be making that same product.

First, I would gather my ingredients as directed by the recipe and measure them in separate containers. If the recipe calls for 12 ingredients, I would then have 12 containers. This ensures that nothing is forgotten.

In the plant the ingredients would go through what is called pre-scale. The ingredients are pulled from the warehouse, measured and segregated into its own bundle away from other ingredients. This process ensures speed to production as well as recording of the lot codes of ingredients allowing the mixer to make each batch continuously and efficiently. This process usually happens the day before production.

I then compared my process for mixing the ingredients to the plants process. From there I compared the rest of the preparation step by step. What I didn't realize at first was that this process of me comparing the manufacturing of the product versus my preparation not only helped me overcome my ignorance of the equipment but actually became my own process for developing new products. It wasn't long before I could easily identify a production processes that would basically dictate capabilities.

This initiative to understanding production, for me, was instrumental in helping with the transition from restaurant setting to production setting. As I traded in one production line for another I have never regretted it. The pulses of the machines are now my adrenalin rush and I make it a point to spend as much time as possible on the floor.

Learning processing would soon become my hobby and I started to develop a process which is now known as the POPS method of product development.

I would attend every production possible. Even on projects I wasn't assigned, to learn as much as I could about the process of mass production whenever I had free time. I felt, and still do, that it was important to be as proficient in the production process as I was in the Gold Standard development process.

I would later go on to create a more proficient process to help capture and process information pertaining to product development.

CHAPTER 2

R&D

The typical structure that incorporates chef's into the food manufacturing and menu development has them reporting into Research & Development. This utilizes the skills of the chef in typically 3 ways.

1. Research of food trends and techniques
2. Development of new products
3. Customer interaction

The first point being research is important to the direction of the brand. It is important for the chef to know what products are best sellers and why as well as what products are poor sellers and why. Typically the direction the chef receives in doing the research comes from marketing. The marketing department is responsible for the placement of the brand and thus uses the R&D department's expertise in areas such as new product launch or scope, refreshing of the menu of offerings and insight into where the culinary trends are in today's marketplace.

As a chef it is sometimes hard to relate to getting food direction from a marketer who usually has a career spanning the marketing of many products and not exclusively in food production. In my opinion, this shouldn't be relevant to your job. I guess I can attribute my attitude as one that was drilled in me while serving in the navy, and that is to follow your orders regardless of who is giving them. It is really not your place to question the projects but rather your place to do your very best as a chef to accomplish the tasks at hand.

Chefs are used to being in charge and this is usually a stumbling block in many a chefs career. I mean being a chef means that you are in charge and usually used to getting things done regardless of feelings. I will touch on this delicate subject later on.

As a chef within the R&D there are 2 key points to focus on when doing your job:

1. Research – Be thorough and precise
2. Development – Strive for perfection

If you follow these 2 simple approaches, your work will reflect your commitment to the projects.

Typically you will spend more time in development than you will in research but a lot of the time a chef spends developing is in the kitchen. Whether it is in your own kitchen or a customer's kitchen, you still get to practice your craft. That, in my opinion, is one of the aspects I enjoy doing what I do.

The same practices are always the order of the day:

- Clean as you go
- Be presentable
- Know your menu
- Never leave the kitchen dirty. I do mean never. Even if there is a kitchen steward there to take care of the space, never ever leave a mess for that person to clean up after you.

These basic beliefs are drilled into our heads over and over as young tadpoles in the kitchen and are usually never ignored but there are some exceptions.

I am still surprised how much some people hate washing dishes. It amazes me that they act as though the dish water will trigger a severe allergic reaction of some sort and they try to pre-occupy themselves with tasks that are more suited to their health. Cleaning as you go is essential to the work we do and not only for obvious sanitary reasons but for setting the example of being a professional chef.

The R&D setting is usually a favorable setting to work in. It is diverse in disciplines such as food science and engineering, which both will have a tremendous influence in culinary development.

The food science part of development is crucial to the success of all projects. All prepared food has to go through a battery of testing in order to ensure it is not only safe for customers to eat but also the product delivers what it was intended to deliver.

All foods go through a process and that process can illustrate you starting with a bounty of vegetables from your garden or frozen lasagna from the grocery store. After picking the vegetables from your garden, you then sort what is edible. After sorting, you then wash, peel if necessary and cut into desired sizes or shapes before cooking. It's no different than making frozen lasagna. Building the lasagna is also a process. You start with a list of ingredients, preparation of the ingredients and then the build and then you pack.

The food scientist will develop the frozen lasagna and all of its components with one goal in mind. They will try to make the absolute best product possible. They will make sure all of the separate ingredients come from a credible source. Once sourced, they will then make sure the ingredients can handle the tolerances demanded from ingredients to function not only in the process but also in the finished good.

Each ingredient has to serve a purpose. I know you probably wonder sometimes when you read the ingredient statement on the back of some packaged foods and question why the list is inundated with ingredients that you can't pronounce.

Those ingredients serve a function. They help with processing, flavor, texture and most importantly shelf life. These are known as functional ingredients.

If a product has to have a shelf life of around a year frozen, you are going to need some help in maintaining its integrity. Not so much to be able to handle the freezing part of the process but most importantly the thaw, reheating and finished product for serving. This is known as a series of abuses that can hinder the beauty of the finished product. A sauce, for example, has to be configured to live up to these abuses that your standard pan sauce doesn't.

Since a flour roux isn't freeze thaw stable, you will then depend on other methods to thicken the sauce. Using starches or gums or a combination of both would be the food scientists approach to development. All while measuring it against your Gold Standard every step of the way.

Operations will also be a big part of your products development process. They are the engineers and plant workers that will manufacture the product. Their job will ensure the safety of the food as well as dictate the speed at which it can be produced. As the old saying goes, "Time is money", and if they can produce 100 units per minute versus 80, it doesn't take long to realize more per minute is far better towards the finished good price.

These are also good examples to show how important it will be for you to be a team player!

Your team isn't always made up of other chefs. It is usually made up of people from a diverse variety of backgrounds and education. Demonstrating teamwork is essential to the success of the project, the product, the brand you represent and the company.

CHAPTER 3

THE POPS APPROACH

I like to consider myself a process driven chef. If there is a process, I follow it, if there isn't a process, well then I develop one. Having spent 10 years in the navy, I would chalk this one up to one of the many things I learned in those 10 years.

Like most chefs, I do have a tendency to take charge. It is, of course, demanded of us whenever we lead the kitchen. We want it to be successful. We want it to be efficient, put out great food and make some money in the process. Well it is no different in the manufacturing world. Everything is just on a bigger scale.

When you walk into a plant for the first time, just think of all the equipment as large versions of what is in your home kitchen. Just more efficient.

From mixers to depositors to ovens and refrigeration, it is only bigger at the end of the day.

The POPS method was created by me to help development chefs with a process if there isn't one already in place. It is an easy transitional method to help you focus and track your development.

It is fondly named after a fellow chef, now passed, named Bill 'Pops' Hahne. He was a passionate product development chef who welcomed me into the fold when I first started in R&D. I miss you brother!

POPS is an acronym for:

PROJECT

OPERATIONS

PROCESS

SUCCESS

Following these 4 simple steps will help develop you into a valuable part of the team.

PROJECT

The idea here is for you to compile a 4 sectioned dossier on each project and compile your notes into each pertaining section for a clear view of the project. This is where you are starting from. Most projects, before they come to you, are usually validated by either sales or marketing as an active interest that the company wishes to pursue. Whether it is a new retail item or a custom foodservice item, first and foremost the company decides whether or not putting valuable resources toward the development of this project will be worth the investment.

Most product development chefs are allotted about 10 – 20 % of their time on what is known as 'Blue Sky' projects. These are ones where you are free to create an item or items that you think will benefit the company without specific direction. I will cover more on this later.

The project starts with what exactly you are making and what department or business unit you are supporting with the project. Projects are usually given a name or number which also tracks the process of development.

I usually start with dividing a legal page of paper into 4 sections with each section representing the 4 parts of POPS. After such, I write in notes and ideas on how best to complete the project. Some projects can have as many of these pages you see fit. There is no qualification for limiting it to just one page. Let your creativity run wild!

Once I know what I am making, it is then time to write in how I will construct the product. Depending on complexity or multi-dimensional products, you will soon be depending upon all of these sections to get a clear picture of the build. There are no rules to completing one section at a time. You will find you have to start a little in each section then build from there.

Projects are usually commissioned in a group setting where you will be filling in pieces of information into each of the 4 sections as the information is shared. For example, what your making, how it will be sold, what line (production facility) it will be made and how much it should cost.

Any and all information shared with you, regardless of which internal department is responsible for completing, is an important part of the project. Take notes on everything. I cannot stress this enough. Your job is not only to develop the Gold Standard but to be an important part of the development process as well as an important part of the development team.

Under the project heading you should write out some recipe ideas. Also look at what ingredients you will need to prepare the item. This is where you will start to develop the Gold Standard.

All too often I have seen development chefs find a recipe, go to the grocery store and pick up canned, frozen or prepared ingredients and start their preparation of the Gold Standard. I cringe just thinking about it.

The Gold Standard should be the purest form possible. Do not, and I repeat, do not cheat yourself, your project or your teammates by taking any shortcuts in this process. If the recipe calls for vegetable stock, then make vegetable stock! Don't buy a can of prepared stock. The flavor isn't a Gold Standard nor is the list of ingredients. If you need to make a reduction or roast bones, then you need to do it right. Buying a prepared concentrate is not the way to go.

Remember, you not only represent the culinary community as a chef, you also represent values that come with being a chef. Shortcuts are neither an option, they should never, never ever even be considered.

Sometimes you will get the opportunity to visit a variety of restaurants in your job. Try to take notes on these visits that will help you develop your Gold Standards. Especially if your aim is to replicate a certain item, break it down as much as possible.

Deconstruct the food on your plate to the bare bones and reverse engineer the several components before you. Take pictures if you need to.

Once your back in your kitchen, start with the very best of ingredients possible and build your recipe one component at a time. This is the part most chefs struggle. Fortunately I first became a pastry chef before moving onto savory. This instilled, at a very early point in my career, to be exact in everything I did. The days of a pinch here, dash here and so on are over. You will need to be methodical in your details. Everything is to be written down and measured usually to the gram. This reminds me, if you don't know your metric system, get to know it. It will be what you will be using from now on.

Once you have all of your ingredients (mise en place) ready to go, get all your cooking equipment together. Now it is important to write down everything you are using but also to keep in mind not to worry about how the plant would do it at this stage. That comes later. Focus on making the best Gold Standard as possible.

When you are preparing your Gold Standard, write down all of your times and temperatures. At this stage there is no such thing as too much information. Every detail needs to be recorded. In most settings you will have a lab book. Use it as much as possible. Sometimes it will be necessary to have one book per project. You will be very surprised how much information is necessary to reach your goals.

Your first development of the Gold Standard is usually you preparing for an internal cutting with the rest of the team assigned to the project. Double check all of the details against what you made and again, take pictures if you have to.

Next step would be to set up an internal cutting with all who are assigned to the project. Once you are ready for that step please keep this in mind. You have spent valuable time researching and preparing this dish. Don't waste all of those efforts by serving this perfect food on polystyrene plates with plastic forks.

Serve the food on proper plates with proper utensils. There is no room for laziness in this position and serving on disposables plates in an effort to save from washing dishes does your food no justice. If you are going to do it, then do it right!

Chapter 4

Operations

Upon completion of an agreed upon Gold Standard, it is now time to replicate within the capabilities of the facility that will be tasked to manufacture the finished good.

You will need to be highly proficient in your company's capabilities. Not only will it help you in your development process but it will help you throughout your career.

Spend as much time in the plants as possible. Get to know how things work from how you scale up raw materials, what batch sizes you can do and most importantly, how can the products be produced with maximum efficiency.

You might be part of this commercialization team and in other circumstances you may not. I will still strongly recommend that you know as much about the capabilities as possible.

The operations part is an important part since this is where you will review the production lines that will produce the finished goods. Each project and each product is unique to itself so adapt to the surroundings and be proactive in the discovery stage of putting the pieces together.

The engineers will configure the lines to meet the needs of the project. They will essentially set up, by paper at first, how the product will be built and packaged. You can learn a lot from these folks to take in as much information as they are willing to share.

Operations will also help you tremendously on costs. If a product is too slow to produce and too labor intensive, your project will never get off the ground. Their plan is to make it as affordable as possible but you have to also understand that you can help them by holding them to the true integrity of the product.

Operations will help you determine whether or not the product you designed can be made in your facility. They will guide you through how each line is set up and whether or not new equipment will need to be fabricated or purchased.

They will also be a tremendous resource throughout each project and be there to help teach you not only on each specific piece of equipment but the plant as a whole.

The operations team is sometimes referred to as technical support.

Chapter 5

Process

This is the stage where you will be working very closely to the food scientist. In some facilities, it may be a food technologist you will work with but either way this stage is an incredibly important one.

This is where you will be translating, so to say, the recipe you developed into a formula. A formula will designate what materials it will take to make the product as well as the costs and procedure assigned to each ingredient.

You will also convert the recipe into percent's of the finished good which achieves 100% of the raw materials then measured against a percentage in loss. Thus giving you a yield in the end of the process.

Converting the recipe to a formula is quite simple once you get the hang of it. In most cases, you will have a structured format in which you start to build what is known as the BOM (build of materials) into the shape of the finished good.

For me, this is an exciting stage in the process. This is where you start to see the project taking shape. You will be sourcing raw materials from suppliers that replicate what you did in your Gold Standard recipe and measure those ingredients against what you started with.

It takes a lot of time at first but once you gain experience and proficiencies on the plant floor, it is a relatively quick process. What takes time is sourcing new ingredients, getting those ingredients spec'd in and qualifying the ingredients within your setting.

Most facilities will have a small pilot plant where you can execute mini trials against the equipment necessary for the build to see if it will work before ordering a truck load of materials to try manufacturing on the larger scale.

It's in the pilot plant where you begin to 'scale up' the product being created.

By scaling up, you are increasing the size of the products raw materials and getting a good sense on the tolerances of the ingredients you have chosen. There is room for errors in this stage so don't be afraid to try new things, new ideas or even a new process.

You should periodically test your formula against your Gold Standard. It will help you measure the progress of the project as well as how far or how close you are to the recipe. This should be a joint effort and used in a sensory type setting to gauge your progress.

Don't be intimidated by negative feedback. This feedback is useful and vital in the process. It helps you improve the project as it progresses as well as improve your confidence in what you are doing.

Gather data and record it. It is important as the project moves forward that you record every detail. It could take months for the project to finally be commercialized and your notes will serve you better than your memory. Once the product is finished you will then have time to review your notes and discard any redundant information. Chances are you will be working on several projects at the same time and each project maybe at different stages in the process. It is sort of like when you were working the line in a restaurant during the busy dinner rush. You plate up orders while you are firing other orders. It is never one in, one out.

Multitasking is nothing new to a chef and it is still very much the plan of the day in product development. It is important to be organized during every part of the product development phase and never to lose focus of each individual task.

With everything else in life, the more experience you gain, the easier it becomes. Almost second nature to initiate, track and execute every task given to the project. Be professional in everything you do and the reward is worth it.

I can't tell you how good it felt to see products on store shelves and on menu boards that I developed. The long hours and grueling schedules were well worth it at the end of the day. You are fulfilling a need in the marketplace. If you take your job seriously and perform at the very best of your ability, customers will continue to use your products for as long as it is available. Never underestimate the choices of the consumer.

Chapter 6

Success

The success of every project is important to the whole team involved. It is not selfish, it is shared. Not just by your R&D team but also the marketing, sales, engineering and most importantly the people on the plant floor making it every day.

As you wrap up your test runs that are now in full production, make it a point to know the folks who are working the line. Try to know their names and work with them during each phase of production. They want to do a good job just like you and they take great pride in what they produce. Share the success with them every chance you get.

I have always made it a point to do my best to make a good impression with the plant workers every chance I got. I am always thankful that when they see me on the floor they are haooy to see me rather than thinking, "Oh man here comes that nothing is ever good enough chef".

I would also make it a point to get with the line supervisors and a few of the line lead workers and keep them abreast of the project, what it entails and what the end product looks like. I would always bring them to the test kitchen the day before, whenever possible, and make the product up for them from raw ingredients to finished product.

I feel it is important for them to know what they will be making and have a visual of the product rather than just read the formula. I had this idea from reading cookbooks when I was young. I liked having pictures of the recipes and since people are very visual, rather than having them just read the recipe, I would demonstrate how it is put together.

By using this method, I increased success. It left less of a chance for error or guesswork and more of a confidence builder among all involved. If it was a raw product we were making, I would cook it off afterword and have them try it. On china not foam plates! I would have sodas and water for them to enjoy and walk them through every phase of the development without divulging any confidential information. It makes for a great setting to get to know the production team as well as make them an important part of the development process.

By practicing making the product with the production crew, I limited waste to a bare minimum. I saved valuable money, resources and time because everybody now knew what the end product was like. On certain complex projects, I would have them rehearse, so to say, making the product. This was an incredible confidence builder. A couple of times they would point out where possible problems could occur and we could fix those problems before the run. Again, saving valuable time, money and resources.

It is not uncommon to see, on product developer's desks and shelves, multiple packaging of the products they developed. For some it can get to the point where they are running out of room but it is a great reminder of success. They are always proud of what was made no matter what the product is. Seeing the packaging and all the pictures and graphics demonstrates the ability to create something from where everything is created, an idea.

When I was in the military success was measured by individuals rank, an individual's awards and an individual's performance. You wore it on your sleeve so to say. Each individual is an important part of the team. It is no different in product development. You as a chef will be working with highly degreed individuals. And just as you are counting on their expertise, they also are counting on yours.

The success of the project depends upon you. If you started with a bad Gold Standard, you have failed the team. You have failed the project and most of all you have failed the company.

In this industry, you will more than likely have more projects fail than get launched. That is just the way it is. But they should fail due to circumstances beyond your control. The customer lost interest. It is not within your current capabilities and there are no monies available in the budget for capital expense.

Customer demands are for something healthier so the project gets shelved. The list goes on. However, the project should never fail due to your inability to deliver the proper Gold Standard. In order to see success and be successful in your product development career, you better know how to cook.

Utilizing the POPS method will help you see success. That is exactly why I designed it. All 4 points will be important to the development process. And as you develop in your career you may configure it to fit your own style of product development.

Meanwhile I would encourage you to follow it as it is until you have the skillset to deviate. It is designed as a building block and not a box.

Chapter 7

Creativity

Throughout your whole culinary career, you have had to be creative. Whether it was for a cost conscious banquet order that still desired that wow effect or utilizing left overs for the staff meal where there is no room for errors. R&D is no different.

You will experience plenty of opportunities to utilize your individual creativity. Like I said earlier, projects are unique to themselves and that demands lots of creativity. From configuring the build of the project to plating up the finished good for some photography beauty shots will demand you to deliver on the creativity side of your art.

I'm a firm believer that in order to explore ones creativity, you will need freedom of expression. Even though your expression in the corporate world is limited to the expression of the company, you will have to limit how far your expression takes you.

Overall, that is not such a bad thing. By focusing in on your brand and what it represents and how that representation connects with the consumer, you will soon find it is an incredibly fun experience. Your creativity should reflect not just the chef's perspective on the end product but how the end user will visually connect to the products presentation. At the end of the day, your goal is to give the end user what THEY want.

As a chef, I am sure you are used to writing your own menus. In R&D the majority of your marching orders come from sales and or marketing. Get used to it, that's just the way it is. Sales will be bringing in requests from either customers or potential customers. This is an important part of what the sales force does and they are your internal customer. Marketing brings in projects that fit the brand as well as fill consumer demands that they usually see fit in providing based upon your brand or perhaps a line extension.

What both of these departments do is incredibly important and I know from a chef's point of view it can sometimes be difficult to fathom getting told what to do by someone other than a fellow chef. It is almost foreign to how we came up in the business but think back to your restaurant days for a minute. As much as we all hated having hamburgers on our hotel restaurant menus we knew we had to have them. Quite simply, you have burgers on the menu because that is exactly what most of the business travelers were comfortable ordering day in and day out. If you didn't have burgers in the menu because you wanted to make a creative approach to what you serve, your GM would be happy to give you lots of creativity free time permanently.

Now getting your orders from outside your department should not and usually will not stifle your creativity. You will be spending lots of time with your marketing team and they will pick your brain and tap into utilizing your creativity to help them represent the brand better.

Just as you have developed relationships with the rest of R&D as well as operations, quality assurance and plant laborers, so also will you need to develop relationships with the sales force and marketing team. Your expertise will be much needed.

It's not uncommon for you to be taken on sales calls with your starched chef coat, sharp knives, big smile and utilizing a creative approach for the customer to use your product. Yes, you will need all of the above and the creative skills to tie your product into practical uses within the customers organization. This requires a good sense of recon and the ability to demonstrate your product at its maximum potential in as many uses as possible.

On these calls, sales take a back seat and you lead the presentation. Whenever possible, I would go over the plan with the sales people before the call so they know exactly what I intend to do. Some help and some don't with prep, shopping etcetera but always plan on doing it solo. This way you're prepared for the presentation and not in the weeds. If you think working a busy dinner rush in the weeds was horrible, wait till you have all eyes on you in a presentation setting with everybody back at your company counting on you to help land the sale. Failure is not an option!

Your creativity will be tested over and over in this circumstance and you need to be prepared. Study your customer. Look at ways your products fit within their brand and for heaven's sake, keep it simple. All too often I have seen presentations that were way over the top as far as prep, labor and food cost and I have always chalked that up to the lack of knowing who your customer is.

Creativity plays a big part in your presentations. I cannot stress this point enough. The importance of creativity within the culinary R&D role is paramount to the success of the company as well as your own personal success throughout your career. Chances are you will be creating recipes for your marketing team's web page, doing features at food shows on both the national and international level and high level sales presentations.

Now if you are in R&D because you like the hours and you get to wear a cool jacket over your business attire, well then you are in it for the wrong reasons. You have to be committed to the craft with vigor and certainty all while representing the future of culinary development. You see, the future of food can and will be at your disposal. If you cannot take on that responsibility then you should consider another path of profession.

And that future depends entirely on your ability to take on highly stressful challenges in a confident manor and have a deep love, respect and passion for food.

Chapter 8

Research

Research, it is the first word in R&D and that is no mistake. It is often overlooked with probably more focus on development, however, no less important.

Your task as a product development chef pertaining to research will have a primary focus on trends, past and present and how your products can fit within those trends. You will also look at new and emerging cooking techniques and how they can be incorporated either within your facility or perhaps within a customer's facility or home kitchen.

Research is important to what your day to day work details. It can come in the form of searching out alternative ingredients or maybe a way to conserve energy, utilize less waste and conserve water. Perhaps you will research food trucks and design a SWOT (strengths, weaknesses, opportunities, threats) analysis to the rest of your team, whom are looking for ways to capitalize on this trend. However the case, you are going to have to be comfortable doing research. Unfortunately most culinary schools don't have a focus on research but typically, as a chef, you should have an uncanny ability to research a lot of what is going on in the culinary world quite comfortably. We are all guilty of it, whether it is patronizing a competitor's restaurant, reading food blogs or subscribing to countless trade magazines, we all do it naturally.

The R&D environment will give you tremendous opportunities to do research. I say, take full advantage of this opportunity and use it towards the benefit of your knowledge in being a passionate product developer.

In order to be a great developer you also have to do your research.

They go hand in hand and with research being 50% of your department's title you can bet it is a serious part of what we do each day.

I would strongly recommend keeping a meticulous log of all of your research. As you well know trends ebb and flow and quite often change each year but never discard what trends don't really have an impact on the immediate year. They do sometimes take a while to gain popularity and should never be overlooked.

Your log should comprise of immediate, intermediate and long term research which will impact your company. Staying relevant in the marketplace is paramount to your success and by doing the research; you are essentially looking into the crystal ball to see what is coming down the road. With any good battle plan, you have to be prepared for the fight. In today's highly competitive market you cannot afford to rest on your current offerings with the confidence that the market will never change. Longevity is only sustained through vision and clarity. In order to have a clear vision of the future, you must plan ahead.

Always refer back to your research and even put little reminders on your calendar if necessary. Focus in on what is relevant to your business and especially to what your competitors are doing. The web is an awesome tool if you know how to use it. With everything at your fingertips, get into the habit of making it a point to watch what is happening around you. Otherwise, it will be happening without you.

You just have to look back at cookbooks in the last 10 to 20 to 30 years and you can witness the transformation of food before your very eyes. We have gone from classical European to pan Asian fusion in that time, for example, and a company that once made meatloaf and mashed potato frozen dinners has added southwestern egg rolls to their portfolio in an effort to stay relevant. Doing your research pays off especially if manufacturing lines have to be reconfigured or plants have to be acquired. This all takes time and with your preparation can pay big dividends in the end.

Speed to market is highly sought after today and the companies that can accomplish capitalizing on speed to market are usually most successful. You will be helping in this effort and by doing so you will need to do your research. Analyze your data and sift through the information with importance. Be very detailed oriented in all aspects of your job and all of that hard work will pay off. Chefs are naturally competitive and so are companies. By using the information you gather, use that to develop some of your Blue Sky projects and help marketing with the critical decisions that they face.

It's a team effort each and every day. Remember you are a part of that team and a valuable one also.

Chapter 9

Development

    The development process within the typical R&D setting is quite similar to most companies within the food manufacturing industry. That could also be said among national chain restaurants. The key is quite simply consistency. A consistent process of execution along with a consistent method to achieve success will result in a consistent product.

    The consistent process is set forth by the head of R&D. Their job is to produce results of each project in a timely and precise manner. Not an easy job at all but one that is incredibly rewarding.

R&D environments are incredibly diverse. Filled with highly educated and very competitive individuals makes for a challenge all in its own for the department head let along managing the budget to ensure you're not overspending on a product that has a low return on investment initially.

The environment is usually fast paced and packed full of meetings from project initiations to project status updates to test runs and so forth. In order to be successful in this highly energized setting you have to be organized. Know every detail of where your projects are and attend every meeting fully prepared in order to meet timelines which are necessary to get the end product to market. The timelines are usually set by the marketing department.

Each project could have different developers on the team or they could have the same. This pretty much depends on the size of the department. Chef's do develop, depending on skillset, so don't be surprised if you are the lead on the project and it is up to you to not only develop the Gold Standard but also commercialize the product.

If you are the developer, use your resources. There are usually an abundant amount of resources to help. Most of all, some great resources come from the supplier's arsenal of their own developers. Their technical people are typically experts in the product they are selling you. They will work with you in developing a specific item for a specific project especially if it needs to be custom formulated.

The success of your project is crucial to the sale of the products they offer to don't be afraid to ask for help or embarrassed because you don't know the application or molecular structure of any given ingredient. The experts are there to help you.

One of the most important parts of development is the secrecy. Intellectual property cannot and should not be shared. Non-disclosure agreements between parties usually cover this but you should still keep your cards very close and never divulge proprietary information. Trade secrets will be a part of your day to day regiment and it is important that you treat them as such. This is why I never open my computer on an airplane and this is why I keep project folders in the office.

Trust is a big part of what you are doing. You are trusted to know how products are made as well as what gives your company a competitive edge above their competitors. There is no room for loud mouths in our business and trust me, this industry is small. You will interact with competitor counterparts in various settings as your career progresses and a good part of those interactions are usually at conferences or food shows which is OK. I'm not saying isolate yourself from the rest of the industry but just be cautious of what you talk about and the word project should never come up in conversation.

As you watch the development each of your projects progress, you will start to develop your best way to manage through all of the important parts of R&D. There are no shortcuts but you will be proficient enough through experience to know what is important and where the challenges will be before they come to you.

The POPS method will help guide you as you see the necessary steps needed to achieve success. You might be strong in only one of the 4 steps at first but with time and experience you should be comfortably proficient in no time. Your success is in your hands and I have only laid the foundation for you to be successful. You will have to build the rest.

Development is just as demanding as it is rewarding. The long hours, endless meetings and minute details that could be costly if overlooked are small in comparison to thousands of people eating your product every day. The gratification is mostly just you and your colleagues celebrating but still, you're celebrating!

This line of work isn't going to land you a James Beard award or a spot on the Food Network but hopefully that is not the reasons you're pursuing a career as a product development chef.

Just as your projects will take time to develop so will your skills within the R&D community. Be organized and professional at all times. Treat each project with the respect it deserves and be an important part of the team. As a chef, you represent the culinary side of the industry that helps shape the way people eat. Never lose sight of the importance of what you do. Even when you're standing over the 3 compartment sink after a marathon in the kitchen, keep your focus. What we do is important. It's not uncommon to us, as chefs, to be on your feet all day and strive for perfection all the while juggling multiple projects at different stages in the process.

Key is, don't dwell on the projects that get killed mid-stream, let them go. Keep a record of the project and file it with all the necessary information if it resurrects again but now focus more intently on the live ones. Continuance improvement will be a big part of each day, so do you're very best in developing the very best product.

Chapter 10

You Are an Artist

As a chef, you are relied upon being an expert in your field. You rose through the ranks most often under harsh circumstances that mold you into what you are today. Whether it be your style, interests or plating ability, you should be passionate about the art of what we do.

As an artist, sitting in a cubicle from 8AM – 5PM Monday through Friday won't sound like fun. Sure, coming from a grind where you don't wrap up work till midnight, this might sound like a much needed break but it can be a struggle for most. Even for me, I sometimes struggle through it. I hear other chefs talk about how much they miss the banter and the intoxication of a dinner rush. Sure, we miss it but this is a new rush. An endless rush. The plant is running constantly and the sound of pneumatic machines has replaced the sound of the ticket machine in your head when you are trying to sleep at night. Instead of wait staff being in your way each night it is now forklifts. Band aids and burn cream has been replaced by sticky notes and dossier of frequent traveler numbers to remember. But you're still an artist.

You create; you style and bring an approach to food development that is valuable to the industry. An artistic view of the food you develop is often overlooked by the glossy picture on the box or on the menu but that is not a deterrent to being an artist.

It is important for you to remember that the arts are synonymous with culinary. Even though you are a developer, you are still an artist. Your mind should be able to construct images of beauty and finesse in every project you work on. Translate those images into products that show your talent. From the Gold Standard phase to the finished goods phase, try to accent the art of what you do and who you are.

Set an example among those around you. An example of the highest caliber that can be recognized in everything you do. Care about the food your developing and show it the respect an artist shows in their work and most of all the respect they show their equipment.

Everything you do should reflect the energy you put forth in striving for perfection. Know your ingredients and put them together artistically. If your project requires a consommé don't show up with bisque because you think it's a better idea. Make the consommé the way you were taught to. Present it properly and deliver on the deliverables.

Demonstrate your artistic ability every chance you get and I assure you, you will get lots of chances to demonstrate but like everybody else in our industry; you are only as good as the last plate you put out. So make it count each and every time.

I love what I do and I consider myself very fortunate to have the opportunity to do it. Product development has been very good to me and I hope I have given back to it respectfully. I also hope this book will serve you well. I wrote it with one goal in mind and that is to keep our profession at the highest of standards. Refer back to these pages as you see a need to and share it with people you hope would benefit from the information provided.

At this point, I could go on and on stressing the importance of what we do but I think I have given you enough information to help get you on track or back on track to being a successful product development chef.

Enjoy the adventure.

Chef Macfarlane has been recipient of many accolades and awards in regards to his work as a product development chef.

He is the founder and Chairman of the Council of Innovative Chefs as well as the developer of the POPS method and Brigade System of Innovation.

POPS is a trademark of the David Food Group and proprietary to his organization.

He is also working on new ways to prepare Scottish cuisine and tirelessly works to promote Scottish cookery. His next project is a cookbook called "Modern Scottish Cuisine".

Cover picture; Welsh Studios.

30175761R00059

Printed in Great Britain
by Amazon